This planner belongs to:

_____

_____

Date

Unless otherwise indicated, all Scripture quotations are taken from the New King James Version. Copyright © 1982 by Thomas Nelson, Inc. Used by permission. All rights reserved.

Verses marked NASB are taken from the New American Standard Bible®, © 1960, 1962, 1963, 1968, 1971, 1972, 1973, 1975, 1977, 1995 by The Lockman Foundation. Used by permission. (www.Lockman.org)

Cover by Bryce Williamson

Cover illustration © Komar art / Shutterstock ; the8monkey / Getty Images

Interior design by Janelle Coury

Author photo © Michael Gomez Photography

THE POWER OF A PRAYING is a registered trademark of The Hawkins Children's LLC. Harvest House Publishers, Inc., is the exclusive licensee of the federally registered trademark THE POWER OF A PRAYING.

Portions of the content were previously published in *The Power of a Praying® Wife, The Power of a Praying® Wife Prayer and Study Guide,* and *The Power of a Praying® Wife Book of Prayers.*

The Power of a Praying® Wife Planner

Copyright © 2019 by Stormie Omartian
Published by Harvest House Publishers
Eugene, Oregon 97408
www.harvesthousepublishers.com

ISBN 978-0-7369-7883-5 (pbk.)

Printed in China

HARVEST HOUSE PUBLISHERS
EUGENE, OREGON

19 20 21 22 23 24 25 26 27 / RDS-JC / 10 9 8 7 6 5 4 3 2 1

Introduction

Every wife is busy. We are establishing and keeping up a home. We are working—whether paid or not—and trying to be the best we can be at everything we do. And if we have children, we are swamped with a list of never-ending tasks that need to be done in order to keep our family healthy, safe, clean, and growing in a positive way. Our challenge is how to find the hours to do all these things and still spend quality time deepening our relationship with the Lord and strengthening our marriage. And somewhere in there we also must take care of ourselves so we, too, can stay healthy, strong, attractive, and able to accomplish all that we want and need to do.

I have found it helps greatly to be organized and to plan ahead. And for me these days, if it isn't written down, it is not happening. That's because there is too much vying for my attention. I need to write down my appointments, obligations, things that must get done, and priorities for each day and make sure I keep them before my eyes so I don't forget. If you need to organize your time in an effective way so as to keep your priorities from being lost in the shuffle, then this planner will help you.

One major priority is to pray for your husband and your marriage every day. In this planner, prayers for him are included each week so you don't have to figure that out. It's designed to help you organize your life so you can include the things that are most important to you. I pray you will enjoy having a daily planner as much as I have.

Stormie Omartian

Lord, I pray for Your blessings and peace to be on the woman who reads and uses this planner. Enable her to know Your plans for her life, while at the same time helping her to make the best use of her time in order to fulfill the purpose You have for her. May this planner make it easier to bring the degree of order and organization into her life that she desires, and reduce any stress a busy life can bring so that it never becomes overwhelming. Teach her to plan her life without neglecting to include certain important things every day that cannot be left to chance—such as praying for her *husband* in order to keep her marriage strong, and scheduling time to read Your Word to keep *herself* spiritually, mentally, and emotionally strong. Remind her to write down everything she needs to do for her own health and sense of well-being. Bring to mind the ways she can pray for her children and/or others close to her whom You have put in her life and heart.

Most of all, I pray that this daughter of Yours will sense Your love for her even in these pages as she spends time prayerfully with You, seeking to know how You want her to order her days. Enable her to live in Your will and experience everything You have for her and her family.

In Jesus' name I pray.

How to Use This Planner

This planner is divided into 52 weeks. Each week you'll find a Scripture for the week, a written prayer for you to pray for your husband, and also a question or two to easily answer that is specific to you or your husband. You don't necessarily have to write down your answer, but it would be good to write a short prayer about it in the space provided so as to remind you to pray more about it.

Periodically, you'll see a blank page called "Prayers for My Husband," where you can jot down things that arise or come to your mind to pray about for him—and for you too. (A big part of praying for your husband is to pray for his wife.)

Another page you will see is "Answers to My Prayers," which gives room for you to jot down answers to any prayers you have prayed. A third type of page is called "Notes." It provides space to jot down anything you want to remember to schedule and do, or just think about for the future.

A great feature in this planner is that you can start it at any time of the year. Just fill in the month at the top of each week and the dates in the boxes provided each day that week. Everything in this planner is for your convenience to help you organize your life and establish your priorities the way you want them to be without taking up too much time out of your day.

Ask, and it will be given to you;
seek, and you will find;
knock, and it will be opened to you.
For everyone who asks receives,
and he who seeks finds,
and to him who knocks it will be opened.

Matthew 7:7-8

God's favorite three-word prayer:

"Change me,
Lord."

Week 1

His Wife

Whatever things you ask when you pray,
believe that you receive them, and you will have them.
And whenever you stand praying, if you have anything against anyone,
forgive him, that your Father in heaven may also forgive you your trespasses.

MARK 11:24-25

Lord, help me to be a good wife. I realize I don't have what it takes to be all You want me to be without Your help.

Take any selfishness and impatience I have and turn them into kindness and understanding so I can be an instrument of restoration.

Take any emotional habits, mind-sets, automatic reactions, and self-protectiveness I may struggle with and make me to be faithful, gentle, forgiving, and self-controlled.

Take any hardness in my heart and give me a new and softer heart. Work in me Your love, peace, and joy (Galatians 5:22-23). I am not able to rise above who I am at this moment. Only You can make changes in me that are lasting.

In Jesus' name I pray.

Read Matthew 12:25 in your Bible. Is there any issue over which you and your husband are seriously divided? List those in a prayer below, asking God to help you work them out peacefully. (For example, "Lord, the areas where my husband and I are divided are [finances, child raising, communication, lifestyle]…")

MON

SAT

TUES

WED

SUN

THUR

FRI

When disappointing things happen in your marriage, thank God for the good qualities in your husband that you most appreciate.

Week 2

His Wife

Through wisdom a house is built
and by understanding it is established;
by knowledge the rooms are filled
with all precious and pleasant riches.

PROVERBS 24:3-4

Lord, I want to confess any time I've been unloving, critical, angry, resentful, disrespectful, or unforgiving toward my husband. Show me those times.

Help me to put aside all hurt, anger, or disappointment I feel and forgive him the way You do—totally and completely, no looking back. Make me to be a tool of reconciliation, peace, and healing in this marriage. Make me to be my husband's helpmate, companion, champion, friend, and support.

Help me to create a peaceful, restful, safe place for him to come home to. Teach me how to take care of myself and stay attractive to him. Grow me into a creative and confident woman who is rich in mind, soul, and spirit. Make me the kind of woman he can be proud to say is his wife.

In Jesus' name I pray.

Look up Proverbs 21:19. Are there any issues in your marriage where you find yourself registering the same complaint or criticism over and over? Write out a prayer asking God to show you when to speak about each matter and when to just keep silent and pray.

MON

SAT

TUES

WED

SUN

THUR

FRI

Ask the Lord to show you how to make your home a safe haven that builds up your family—a place where creativity flows and communication is ongoing.

Week 3

His Wife

Be kind to one another, tenderhearted,
forgiving one another, even as God in Christ forgave you.

EPHESIANS 4:32

Lord, I lay all my expectations at Your cross. I release my husband from the burden of fulfilling me in areas where I should be looking to You.

Help me to accept him the way he is and not try to change him. I realize that in some ways he may never change, but at the same time, I release him to change in ways I never thought he could.

I leave any changing that needs to be done in Your hands, fully accepting that neither of us is perfect and never will be.

Only You, Lord, are perfect, and I look to You to perfect us. May we be "perfectly joined together in the same mind and in the same judgment" (1 Corinthians 1:10).

In Jesus' name I pray.

Read Psalm 6:5 and underline it in your Bible. Do you have expectations of your husband that he is not living up to? What are they? Write out a prayer asking God to show you where your expectations of your husband don't coincide with the reality of who he is. Tell God you will put all your expectations on *Him* so *He* can meet your needs.

MONTH: DATE:

MON

SAT

TUES

WED

SUN

THUR

FRI

Take your needs to God in prayer and look to *Him* for the answers. Be specific.

Week 4

His Wife

Let us not grow weary while doing good,
for in due season we shall reap
if we do not lose heart.

GALATIANS 6:9

Lord, teach me how to pray for my husband and make my prayers a true language of love. Where love has died, create new love between us. Show me what unconditional love really is and how to communicate it in a way he can clearly perceive.

Bring unity between us so that we can be in agreement about everything (Amos 3:3). May the God of patience and comfort grant us to be like-minded toward one another, according to Christ Jesus (Romans 15:5).

Make us a team, not pursuing separate, competitive, or independent lives, but working together, overlooking each other's faults and weaknesses for the greater good of the marriage. Help us to pursue the things that make for peace and the things by which one may edify another (Romans 14:19).

In Jesus' name I pray.

Read Matthew 19:3-6 in your Bible. Do you believe that you and your husband are one in the sight of God? Are there places in your marriage where you and your husband are not working together as a team? List those areas, and then write out a prayer asking God to make you and your husband more unified. Ask Him to show you what you can do to facilitate that unity.

MONTH: DATE:

MON

SAT

TUES

WED

SUN

THUR

FRI

Prayer gives rise to love,
love inspires more prayer,
which in turn gives rise
to more love. When you
pray for someone, you
grow to love them more.

Prayers for My Husband

Answers to My Prayers

Prayer is the ultimate
love language.
It communicates love
in ways we often can't.

Week 5

His Work

Do you see a man who excels in his work?
He will stand before kings;
he will not stand before unknown men.

PROVERBS 22:29

Lord, I pray that You would bless the work of my husband's hands. May his labor bring not only favor, success, and prosperity, but great fulfillment as well. If the work he is doing is not in line with Your perfect will for his life, reveal that to him. Show him what he should do differently and guide him down the right path.

Give him strength, faith, and a vision for the future so he can rise above any propensity for laziness. May he never run from work out of fear, selfishness, or a desire to avoid responsibility.

On the other hand, help him to see that he doesn't have to work himself to death for man's approval. Give him the ability to enjoy his success without striving for more. Help him to excel, but free him from the pressure to do so.

In Jesus' name I pray.

Read Ecclesiastes 3:12-13. Is your husband's work fulfilling to him? Does he enjoy the good of his labor? Write out a prayer asking God to help your husband find fulfillment in his work, whether it means moving him into something different than what he is doing now or giving him a new sense of purpose about the work he already has.

MONTH: DATE:

MON

TUES

WED

THUR

FRI

SAT

SUN

God recognizes that a man's work is a source of fulfillment to him. He says there is nothing better than for a man to "enjoy the good of all his labor—it is the gift of God" (Ecclesiastes 3:13).

Week 6

His Work

Let the beauty of the LORD our God be upon us,
and establish the work of our hands for us;
yes, establish the work of our hands.

PSALM 90:17

God, I pray that You will be Lord over my husband's work. May he bring You into every aspect of it. Give him enough confidence in the gifts You've placed in him to be able to seek, find, and do good work. Open doors of opportunity for him that no man can close.

Develop his skills so that they grow more valuable with each passing year. Show me what I can do to encourage him. I pray that his work will be established, secure, successful, satisfying, and financially rewarding.

Let him be like a tree planted by the stream of Your living water, which brings forth fruit in due season. May he never wither under pressure but grow strong and prosper (Psalm 1:3).

In Jesus' name I pray.

Is your husband living up to his potential? Does he have gifts and talents that are not being used or are not being used to the glory of God? Does he know what his gifts and talents are? Write out your answers in a prayer asking God to open up doors for your husband that utilize the gifts God has placed in him.

MON

TUES

WED

THUR

FRI

SAT

SUN

Your prayers can help your husband understand that the true meaning of life doesn't come from work. It comes from following God.

Week 7

His Finances

Do not seek what you should eat or what you
should drink, nor have an anxious mind.
For all these things the nations of the world seek after,
and your Father knows that you need these things.
But seek the kingdom of God,
and all these things shall be added to you.

LUKE 12:29-31

Lord, I commit our finances to You. Be in charge of them and use them for Your purposes.

May my husband and I be good stewards of all that You give us and walk in total agreement as to how it is to be disbursed. I pray that we will learn to live free of burdensome debt.

Where we have not been wise, bring restoration and give us guidance. Show me how I can help increase our finances and not decrease them unwisely. Help us to remember that all we have belongs to You and to be grateful for it.

In Jesus' name I pray.

Do you feel that your husband makes financially sound decisions? Write out your answer in a prayer asking God to give you and your husband wisdom as to how to handle your finances.

MON

SAT

TUES

WED

SUN

THUR

FRI

So many money problems can be solved by putting all finances under God's covering and doing what He says to do with them.

Week 8

His Finances

My God shall supply all your need
according to His riches in glory by Christ Jesus.

Philippians 4:19

Lord, I pray that (husband's name) will have wisdom to handle money wisely. Help him make good decisions as to how he spends. Show him how to plan for the future. Teach him to give as You have instructed in Your Word.

I pray that he will find the perfect balance between spending needlessly and being miserly. May he always be paid well for the work he does, and may his money not be stolen, lost, devoured, destroyed, or wasted. Multiply it so that what he makes will go a long way.

I pray that he will not be anxious about finances but will seek Your kingdom first, knowing that as he does, we will have all we need (Luke 12:31).

In Jesus' name I pray.

Read Luke 12:29-31. Does your husband suffer from anxiety about finances? In light of these verses, what should he be doing about any stress he feels? Write out a prayer about this.

MON

SAT

TUES

WED

SUN

THUR

FRI

God's desire is to bless those who have obedient, grateful, and giving hearts, whose true treasure is in the Lord.

Prayers for My Husband

Answers to My Prayers

God gives great blessings to those who seek Him and live in obedience to His ways.

Week 9

His Sexuality

Do you not know that your body is the temple of the Holy Spirit
who is in you, whom you have from God,
and you are not your own? For you were bought
at a price; therefore glorify God in your body and
in your spirit, which are God's.

1 Corinthians 6:19-20

Lord, bless my husband's sexuality and make it an area of great fulfillment for him. Restore what needs to be restored, balance what needs to be balanced. Protect us from apathy, disappointment, criticism, busyness, unforgiveness, deadness, or disinterest.

I pray that we will make time for one another, communicate our true feelings openly, and remain sensitive to what each other needs. Keep us sexually pure in mind and body, and close the door to anything lustful outside of our marriage that seeks to encroach upon us.

Deliver us from the bondage of any past mistakes we have made. Remove completely the effect of all sexual experience—in thought or deed—that has ever happened to us outside of our relationship. Purify us by the power of Your Spirit.

In Jesus' name I pray.

List the top ten priorities in your life. These are the things that occupy your time, attention, and energy, such as children, work, friends, church activities, and so on. In this list, where does your relationship with your husband fall? What does this list reveal to you about your priorities? Write out a prayer asking God to help you and your husband keep your priorities in right order.

MONTH: **DATE:**

MON

TUES

WED

THUR

FRI

SAT

SUN

Sex between a husband
and a wife is God's idea.
It's important to make
intimacy a matter of
priority in your marriage.

Week 10

His Sexuality

*The body is not for sexual immorality
but for the Lord, and the Lord for the body.*

1 Corinthians 6:13

Lord, take away anyone or anything from my husband's life that would inspire temptation to infidelity. Help him to "abstain from sexual immorality" (1 Thessalonians 4:3).

I pray that we will desire each other and no one else. Show me how to make myself attractive and desirable to him and to be the kind of partner he needs. I pray that neither of us will ever be tempted to think about seeking fulfillment elsewhere. I realize that an important part of my ministry to my husband is sexual. Help me to never use it as a weapon or a means of manipulation by giving and withholding it for selfish reasons.

I commit this area of our lives to You, Lord. Make it all that You created it to be.

In Jesus' name I pray.

Has your husband ever been tempted toward infidelity? Have you? Has that temptation been acted upon? If yes, how has that affected the way you relate to each other? If no, how do you keep yourselves from temptation? Write out a prayer asking God to protect both of you from immorality.

MONTH: DATE:

MON

TUES

WED

THUR

FRI

SAT

SUN

When we're married, our bodies are not our own. We *owe* each other physical attention, and we're not to deprive one another.

Week 11

His Affection

Husbands ought to love their own wives as their own bodies;
he who loves his wife loves himself. For no one ever hated his own flesh,
but nourishes and cherishes it, just as the Lord does the church.

EPHESIANS 5:28-29

Lord, I pray for open physical affection between my husband and me. Enable each of us to lay aside self-consciousness or apathy and be effusive in our display of love for each other.

Help us to demonstrate how much we care for and value each other. Remind us throughout each day to affectionately touch one another in some way.

Help us to not be cold, undemonstrative, uninterested, or remote. Enable us to be warm, tender, compassionate, and loving. Break through any hard-headedness on our part that refuses to change and grow. If one of us is less affectionate to the other's detriment, bring us into balance.

Change any habits of indifference we have so that we can become the husband and wife You called us to be.

In Jesus' name I pray.

Read 1 Corinthians 7:3 in your Bible. Do you feel your husband is affectionate enough toward you? Write out your answer in a prayer. (For example, "Lord, help me [my husband] to be more affectionate toward my husband [me].")

MON

TUES

WED

THUR

FRI

SAT

SUN

The most joyful women
carry the Word of God
in their heart and let it
mold their character.

Week 12

His Temptations

No temptation has overtaken you except such as is common to man;
but God is faithful, who will not allow you to be tempted
beyond what you are able, but with the temptation
will also make the way of escape, that you may be able to bear it.

1 Corinthians 10:13

Lord, I pray that You would strengthen my husband to resist any temptation that comes his way. Deliver him from evils such as adultery, pornography, drugs, alcohol, gambling, and perversion. Remove temptation especially in the area of (name of specific temptation).

Make him strong where he is weak. Help him to rise above anything that seeks to establish a stronghold in his life. Lord, You've said that "whoever has no rule over his own spirit is like a city broken down, without walls" (Proverbs 25:28).

I pray that (husband's name) will not be broken down by the power of evil but raised up by the power of God. Help him to take charge over his own spirit and have self-control to resist anything and anyone who becomes a temptation.

In Jesus' name I pray.

Read Mark 14:38. Even if your husband is not habitually tempted by anything in particular, temptation is always a possibility for anyone, especially where our flesh is weakest. Does your husband have a weakness in the flesh that you feel *could* become a snare from the enemy? Write out a prayer asking God to protect your husband in this area and show you anything you need to see.

MONTH: DATE:

MON

TUES

WED

THUR

FRI

SAT

SUN

Open confession before God and other believers does more to minimize the power of the tempter than anything else.

Prayers for My Husband

Answers to My Prayers

The most important "good" a wife can do for her husband is pray for him consistently every day.

Week 13

His Mind

Though we walk in the flesh, we do not war according to the flesh.
For the weapons of our warfare are not carnal but mighty in God
for pulling down strongholds, casting down arguments
and every high thing that exalts itself against the knowledge of God,
bringing every thought into captivity to the obedience of Christ.

2 Corinthians 10:3-5

Lord, I pray for Your protection on my husband's mind. Shield him from the lies of the enemy. Help him to clearly discern between Your voice and any other, and show him how to take every thought captive as You have instructed us to do.

May he thirst for Your Word and hunger for Your truth so that he can recognize wrong thinking. Give him strength to resist lying thoughts. Where the enemy's lies have already invaded his thoughts, cleanse his mind. Lord, You have given us authority "over all the power of the enemy" (Luke 10:19).

By that authority given to me in Jesus Christ, I speak that the lies of the enemy have no power over my husband's mind, because You, God, have given (husband's name) a sound mind.

In Jesus' name I pray.

Do you believe that God has given you all authority over the enemy on behalf of your husband? Write out a prayer asking God to reveal any lies you feel your husband is believing. (For example, "Lord, I see that my husband feels doubt about his own worth. Open his eyes to see the truth about…")

MON

SAT

TUES

WED

SUN

THUR

FRI

The two most powerful weapons against the attack of lies upon your husband's mind are the *Word of God* and *praise*.

Week 14

His Mind

To be carnally minded is death,
but to be spiritually minded is life and peace.

ROMANS 8:6

Lord, I pray that my husband will not entertain confusion in his mind but will live in clarity. Keep him from being tormented with impure, evil, negative, or sinful thoughts. Enable him to be transformed by the renewing of his mind (Romans 12:2).

Help him to be anxious for nothing, but in everything by prayer and supplication, with thanksgiving, let his requests be made known to You; and may Your peace, which surpasses all understanding, guard his heart and mind through Christ Jesus (Philippians 4:6-7).

And finally, whatever things are true, noble, just, pure, lovely, of good report, having virtue, or anything praiseworthy, let him think on these things (Philippians 4:8). I pray the same for myself.

In Jesus' name I pray.

Read 1 Corinthians 2:16. Write out this verse as a prayer over your husband to help him bring every thought under God's control. Then thank God for what we have in Christ. (For example, "Lord, I thank You that we have the mind of Christ. I pray that my husband will fully recognize that.")

MONTH: DATE:

MON

SAT

TUES

WED

SUN

THUR

FRI

Speak praise to God
for the sound mind He
has given you and your
husband, and pray he will
be able to think clearly
about what he will and
will not allow into it.

Week 15

His Fears

The angel of the LORD encamps all around those
who fear Him, and delivers them.

PSALM 34:7

Lord, You've said in Your Word that "there is no fear in love; but perfect love casts out fear, because fear involves torment. But he who fears has not been made perfect in love" (1 John 4:18).

I pray You will perfect my husband in Your love so that tormenting fear finds no place in him. I know You have not given him a spirit of fear. You've given him power, love, and a sound mind (2 Timothy 1:7).

I pray in the name of Jesus that fear will not rule over my husband. Instead, may Your Word penetrate every fiber of his being, convincing him that Your love for him is far greater than anything he faces, and nothing can separate him from it.

In Jesus' name I pray.

Do you know of any fears your husband has? Do you share any of those same fears? Write out your answers as a prayer asking God to deliver him—and you, if you share those same fears—from all fear.

MONTH: DATE:

MON

SAT

TUES

WED

SUN

THUR

FRI

Having the fear of God—
which means fearing what
your life would be like
without Him—is the only
kind of fear we're supposed
to have. In this case, "fear"
means "reverence."

Week 16

His Fears

Fear not, for I am with you; be not dismayed,
for I am your God. I will strengthen you, yes,
I will help you, I will uphold you with
My righteous right hand.

Isaiah 41:10

Lord, I pray that my husband will acknowledge You as a Father whose love is unfailing, whose strength is without equal, and in whose presence there is nothing to fear. Deliver him this day from fear that destroys and replace it with godly fear (Jeremiah 32:40).

Teach him Your way, O Lord. Help him to walk in Your truth. Unite his heart to fear Your name (Psalm 86:11).

May he have no fear of men but rise up and boldly say, "The LORD is my helper; I will not fear. What can man do to me?" (Hebrews 13:6). "How great is Your goodness, which You have laid up for those who fear You" (Psalm 31:19).

In Jesus' name I pray.

Read Psalm 27:1. When God is your strength, of whom should you be afraid? Write out your answer as a prayer. (For example, "Lord, I thank You that You are not only 'the light of my life,' but You're also '_____.' I pray You will be all that to both me and my husband.")

MONTH:　　　　　　　　　　**DATE:**

MON

TUES

WED

THUR

FRI

SAT

SUN

When we seek God,
He hears us and delivers
us from all of our fears.
He will do the same for
your husband when
you pray for him.

Week 17

His Fears

I sought the LORD, and He heard me,
and delivered me from all my fears.

PSALM 34:4

I say to you, (husband's name), "Be strong, do not fear! Behold, your God will come with vengeance, with the recompense of God; He will come and save you" (Isaiah 35:4).

"In righteousness you shall be established; you shall be far from oppression, for you shall not fear" (Isaiah 54:14).

"You shall not be afraid of the terror by night, nor of the arrow that flies by day, nor of the pestilence that walks in darkness, nor of the destruction that lays waste at noonday" (Psalm 91:5-6).

May the Spirit of the Lord rest upon you, "the Spirit of wisdom and understanding, the Spirit of counsel and might, the Spirit of knowledge and of the fear of the LORD" (Isaiah 11:2).

In Jesus' name I pray.

Read Psalm 34:9-10. In light of these verses, how could you pray for your husband whenever he has fear about not having enough?

MONTH: **DATE:**

MON

TUES

WED

THUR

FRI

SAT

SUN

Pray for the comforting,
securing, perfect love
of the Lord to surround
your husband and deliver
him from all his fears.

Prayers for My Husband

Answers to My Prayers

Great things can happen in our lives when we keep praying and don't allow fear to rule the situation.

Week 18

His Purpose

[May] the God of our Lord Jesus Christ, the Father
of glory…give to you the spirit of wisdom and
revelation in the knowledge of Him,
the eyes of your understanding being enlightened;
that you may know what is the hope of His calling,
what are the riches of the glory of His inheritance in the saints.

EPHESIANS 1:17-18

Lord, I pray that (husband's name) will clearly hear the call You have on his life. Help him to realize who he is in Christ and give him certainty he was created for a high purpose. Enable him to walk worthy of his calling and remind him of what You've called him to be. Don't let him get sidetracked with things that are unessential to Your purpose.

Strike down discouragement so that it will not defeat him. Lift his eyes above the circumstances of the moment so he can see the purpose for which You created him. Give him patience to wait for Your perfect timing.

I pray that the desires of his heart will not be in conflict with the desires of Yours. May he seek You for direction and hear when You speak to his soul.

In Jesus' name I pray.

Do you have a sense of what your husband's purpose in life is, or who God created him to be? Write out your answer to this question in a prayer. (For example, "Lord, show my husband what his purpose and calling is. Show me as well…")

MON

TUES

WED

THUR

FRI

SAT

SUN

When your husband discovers what his purpose and calling are, and he is doing what he was created to do, he will become what he was created to be and find peace and fulfillment.

Week 19

His Choices

A wise man will hear and increase learning,
and a man of understanding will attain wise counsel.

PROVERBS 1:5

God, fill my husband with the fear of the Lord and give him wisdom for every decision he makes. May he reverence You and Your ways and seek to know Your truth. Give him discernment to make decisions based on Your revelation. Help him to make godly choices and keep him from doing anything foolish.

I pray that he will listen to godly counselors and not be a man who is unteachable. Instruct him even as he is sleeping (Psalm 16:7), and in the morning, I pray he will do what's right rather than follow the leading of his own flesh. May he not buy into the foolishness of this world but keep his eyes on You and have ears to hear Your voice.

In Jesus' name I pray.

Read Proverbs 1:7. Does your husband seek God before making decisions? Does he wait for God's leading before acting? Write out a prayer for your husband in light of this Scripture and your answers to these questions. (For example, "Lord, I pray that my husband will…")

MON

TUES

WED

THUR

FRI

SAT

SUN

So much of our lives are
affected by decisions
our husbands make. We
are wise to pray that
they make good ones.

Week 20

His Health

I have heard your prayer, I have seen your tears;
surely I will heal you.

2 KINGS 20:5

Lord, I pray for Your healing touch on (husband's name). Make every part of his body function the way You designed it to.

Wherever there is anything out of balance, set it in perfect working order. Heal him of any disease, illness, injury, infirmity, or weakness.

Strengthen his body to successfully endure his workload, and when he sleeps may he wake up completely rested, rejuvenated, and refreshed.

I pray that he will have the desire to take care of his body, to eat the kind of food that brings health, to get regular exercise, and avoid anything that would be harmful to him. Help him to understand that his body is Your temple and he should care for it as such (1 Corinthians 3:16).

In Jesus' name I pray.

Have you tried to get your husband to do things for his health, but he just won't do them? How does that make you feel when he won't take your suggestions to heart? What do you think he should be doing for his health? Write out your answers in a prayer. (For example, "Lord, with regard to my husband's health, I pray that he would…")

MON

TUES

WED

THUR

FRI

SAT

SUN

Pray for your husband
to learn to take proper
care of himself, and if
he becomes ill, pray
for him to be healed.

Week 21

His Protection

He who dwells in the secret place of the Most High
shall abide under the shadow of the Almighty.
I will say to the LORD, "He is my refuge and my fortress;
my God, in Him I will trust."

PSALM 91:1-2

Lord, I pray that You would protect (husband's name) from any accidents, diseases, dangers, or evil influences. Keep him safe, especially in cars and planes. Hide him from violence and the plans of evil people. Wherever he walks, secure his steps. Keep him on Your path so that his feet don't slip (Psalm 17:5).

If his foot does slip, hold him up by Your mercy (Psalm 94:18). Give him the wisdom and discretion that will help him walk safely and not fall into danger (Proverbs 3:21-23).

Save him from any plans of the enemy that seek to destroy his life (Psalm 103:4). Preserve his going out and his coming in from this time forth and even forevermore (Psalm 121:8).

In Jesus' name I pray.

Do you see any possible dangers in your husband's life that need to be covered in prayer (travel in cars or airplanes or dangers at work)? List them in a prayer and be specific. (For example, "Lord, I pray You would protect my husband. I am especially concerned when he…")

MON

TUES

WED

THUR

FRI

SAT

SUN

Prayer for your husband's protection needs to be frequent and ongoing. You never know when it might be needed in a battlefield.

Prayers for My Husband

Answers to My Prayers

Give me Your heart
for my husband, Lord,
and help me to see him
the way You see him—
as Your beloved son.

Week 22

His Trials

You have been grieved by various trials,
that the genuineness of your faith, being much more precious
than gold that perishes, though it is tested by fire,
may be found to praise, honor, and glory at the revelation of Jesus Christ.

1 Peter 1:6-7

Lord, You alone know the depth of the burden my husband carries. I may understand the specifics, but You have measured the weight of it on his shoulders.

I've not come to minimize what You are doing in his life, for I know You work great things in the midst of trials. Nor am I trying to protect him from what he must face.

I only want to support him so that he will get through this battle as the winner. Help him to remember that "the steps of a good man are ordered by the Lord, and He delights in his way. Though he fall, he shall not be utterly cast down; for the Lord upholds him with His hand" (Psalm 37:23-24).

In Jesus' name I pray.

Read Romans 8:28. Do you really believe that? Is your faith strong enough to help your husband find the good in tough times? Are you willing to pray him through any trial? Write out your answers in a prayer. (For example, "Lord, I believe that You work everything out for good for those who love You. Help my husband to…")

MON

SAT

TUES

WED

SUN

THUR

FRI

Your prayers can greatly
help your husband
maintain a positive
outlook of gratitude, hope,
patience, and peace in
the midst of a trial.

Week 23

His Trials

You, who have shown me great and severe troubles,
shall revive me again, and bring me up again from the depths of the earth.
You shall increase my greatness, and comfort me on every side.

PSALM 71:20-21

Lord, You are our refuge and strength, a very present help in trouble (Psalm 46:1). You have invited us to "come boldly to the throne of grace, that we may obtain mercy and find grace to help in time of need" (Hebrews 4:16).

I come before Your throne and ask for grace for my husband. Strengthen his heart for this battle and give him patience to wait on You (Psalm 27:1-4).

Build him up so that no matter what happens he will be able to stand strong through it. Help him to be always "rejoicing in hope, patient in tribulation, continuing steadfastly in prayer" (Romans 12:12).

Give him endurance to run the race and not give up, for You have said that "a righteous man may fall seven times and rise again" (Proverbs 24:16).

In Jesus' name I pray.

Do you believe your prayers can make a difference in how your husband responds to trials? How so? Write out your answer in a prayer. (For example, "Lord, I believe my prayers for my husband can…")

MON

SAT

TUES

WED

SUN

THUR

FRI

Whether it feels like it or
not, when we serve God,
His love attends every
moment of our lives—even
the toughest, loneliest, most
painful, and desperate.

Week 24

His Integrity

The integrity of the upright will guide them,
but the perversity of the unfaithful will destroy them.

PROVERBS 11:3

Lord, I pray that You would make my husband a man of integrity, according to Your standards.

Give him strength to say yes when he should say yes and courage to say no when he should say no. Enable him to stand for what he knows is right and not waver under pressure from the world.

Don't let him be a man who is "always learning and never able to come to the knowledge of the truth" (2 Timothy 3:7).

Give him instead a teachable spirit that is willing to listen to the voice of wisdom and grow in Your ways.

In Jesus' name I pray.

Is the man your husband appears to be to other people the same or different than the man you know him to be in private? How so? Write out your answers in a prayer. (For example, "Lord, when my husband is with other people, he is…") Tell God what you would like to see Him do in your husband.

MON

TUES

WED

THUR

FRI

SAT

SUN

Integrity is not just what you *appear* to be when all eyes are on you. It's also who you *are* when no one is looking.

Prayers for My Husband

Answers to My Prayers

God helps us to have integrity that will always guide us to do the right thing.

31 Areas of Prayer Focus

Try this little experiment and see what happens. Pray for your husband every day for a month using one of the 31 areas of prayer focus listed below. Pray a focus a day. Ask God to pour out His blessings on your husband and fill you both with His love. See if your heart doesn't soften toward him. Notice if his attitude toward you changes as well. Observe whether your relationship isn't running more smoothly. If you have trouble making that kind of prayer commitment, think of it from the Lord's perspective. Seeing your husband through God's eyes—not just as your husband, but as God's child, a son whom the Lord loves—can be a great revelation. If someone called and asked you to pray for his or her son, you would do it, wouldn't you? Well, God is asking.

His Wife	His Protection	His Walk
His Work	His Trials	His Talk
His Finances	His Integrity	His Repentance
His Sexuality	His Reputation	His Deliverance
His Affection	His Priorities	His Obedience
His Temptations	His Relationships	His Self-Image
His Mind	His Fatherhood	His Faith
His Fears	His Past	His Hearing
His Purpose	His Attitude	His Future
His Choices	His Marriage	
His Health	His Emotions	

Notes

Proverbs 31 List

Read Proverbs 31:10-31.
Ask yourself the following questions without expecting perfection:

Are you a trustworthy wife?

Yes _____   Need Improvement _____

Are you an asset to your husband?

Yes _____   Need Improvement _____

Do you work diligently to make a home in which he can be comfortable and happy?

Yes _____   Need Improvement _____

Are you careful and wise with money?

Yes _____   Need Improvement _____

Do you take care of your physical health and appearance?

Yes _____   Need Improvement _____

Are you a giving person?

Yes _____   Need Improvement _____

Are you prepared for the future?

Yes _____   Need Improvement _____

Do you make sure your family members have their needs met?

Yes _____   Need Improvement _____

Do you generally move in wisdom?

        Yes _____   Need Improvement _____

Are you always loving and kind?

        Yes _____   Need Improvement _____

Is your relationship with the Lord alive, intimate, growing, and strong?

        Yes _____   Need Improvement _____

Without being hard on yourself, write out a prayer asking God to help you with each area in which you need to improve, and to enable you to become the wife He wants you to be.

Week 25

His Reputation

Hide me from the secret plots of the wicked,
from the rebellion of the workers of iniquity,
who sharpen their tongue like a sword, and bend
their bows to shoot their arrows—bitter words.

PSALM 64:2-3

Lord, I pray that (husband's name) will have a reputation that is untarnished. I know that a man is often valued "by what others say of him" (Proverbs 27:21), so I pray that he will be respected in our town and people will speak highly of him.

You've said in Your Word that "a curse without cause shall not alight" (Proverbs 26:2). I pray that there would never be any reason for bad things to be said of my husband. Keep him out of legal entanglements. Protect us from lawsuits and criminal proceedings. Deliver him from his enemies, O God. Defend him from those who rise up to do him harm (Psalm 59:1).

In You, O Lord, we put our trust. Let us never be put to shame (Psalm 71:1).

In Jesus' name I pray.

Do you sense influences around your husband that are trying to persuade him away from staying on the right path? If so, write out a prayer asking God to remove such bad influences. If not, ask God to continue to keep bad influences out of your husband's life.

MON

SAT

TUES

WED

SUN

THUR

FRI

A reputation isn't something to be taken lightly. A good name is to be chosen over great riches (Proverbs 22:1) and is better than "precious ointment" (Ecclesiastes 7:1).

Week 26

His Reputation

Do not let me be ashamed, O LORD, for I have called upon You…
Let the lying lips be put to silence, which speak insolent things proudly
and contemptuously against the righteous.

PSALM 31:17-18

Lord, Your Word says that "a good tree cannot bear bad fruit, nor can a bad tree bear good fruit. Every tree that does not bear good fruit is cut down and thrown into the fire" (Matthew 7:18-19).

I pray that my husband will bear good fruit out of the goodness that is within him, and that he will be known by the good that he does.

May the fruits of honesty, trustworthiness, and humility sweeten all his dealings so that his reputation will never be spoiled. Preserve his life from the enemy, hide him from the secret counsel of the wicked. Pull him out of any net which has been laid for him (Psalm 31:4).

If You are for us, who can be against us? (Romans 8:31).

In Jesus' name I pray.

Three ways our reputations can be ruined are: 1) by the wrong things we do, 2) by the people with whom we are associated, or 3) by disparaging words spoken about us. Have any of these three ever happened to you or your husband? Write out your answer as a prayer asking God to protect your husband's and your reputations.

MON

TUES

WED

THUR

FRI

SAT

SUN

Prayer for your husband's reputation should be an ongoing process. You never know when the plans of the enemy will try to encroach upon your life.

Week 27

His Reputation

Blessed are you when they revile and persecute you,
and say all kinds of evil against you falsely for My sake.
Rejoice and be exceedingly glad, for great is your reward in heaven,
for so they persecuted the prophets who were before you.

MATTHEW 5:11-12

Lord, I pray You would keep my husband safe from the evil of gossiping mouths. Where there has been ill spoken of him, touch the lips of those who speak it with Your refining fire. Let them be ashamed and brought to confusion who seek to destroy his life; let them be driven backward and brought to dishonor who wish him evil (Psalm 40:14).

May he trust in You and not be afraid of what man can do to him (Psalm 56:11). For You have said whoever believes in You will not be put to shame (Romans 10:11).

Lead him, guide him, and be his mighty fortress and hiding place. May his light so shine before men that they see his good works and glorify You, Lord (Matthew 5:16).

In Jesus' name I pray.

Gossip can destroy reputations quickly. Write out a prayer asking God to protect both you and your husband from it. And if it has already happened to either or both of you, ask God to redeem this situation and restore your good reputation.

MON

SAT

TUES

WED

SUN

THUR

FRI

A good reputation is something to value and respect. It is worth protecting in prayer.

Week 28

His Priorities

Seek first the kingdom of God and His righteousness,
and all these things shall be added to you.

MATTHEW 6:33

Lord, I pray for my husband's priorities to be in perfect order. Be Lord and Ruler over his heart. Help him to choose a simplicity of life that will allow him to have time alone with You, Lord, a place to be quiet in Your presence every day. Speak to him about making Your Word, prayer, and praise a priority. Enable him to place me and our children in greater prominence in his heart than career, friends, and activities.

I pray he will seek You first and submit his all to You, for when he does, I know the other pieces of his life will fit together perfectly.

Help me to properly put my husband before children, work, family, friends, activities, and interests too.

Show me what I can do right now to demonstrate to him that he has this position in my heart.

In Jesus' name I pray.

Read Philippians 2:4. Does your husband look out for the interests of his family before himself? Do you feel he puts the interests of other people before his own family? How does this affect your family? Write out your answers in a prayer regarding how you feel about your husband's priorities.

MON

TUES

WED

THUR

FRI

SAT

SUN

If you want your husband to place you as a priority over work, children, friends, and activities, you need to do the same for him.

Prayers for My Husband

Answers to My Prayers

....

....

....

....

....

....

....

....

....

....

....

....

....

....

....

....

Let your husband know
you are praying for
him and ask him what
he specifically wants
you to pray about.

Week 29

His Relationships

A new commandment I give to you, that you love one another;
as I have loved you, that you also love one another.
By this all will know that you are My disciples,
if you have love for one another.

JOHN 13:34-35

Lord, I pray for (husband's name) to have good, godly male friends with whom he can openly share his heart. May they be trustworthy men of wisdom who will speak truth into his life and not just say what he wants to hear (Proverbs 28:23).

Give him the discernment to separate himself from anyone who will not be a good influence (1 Corinthians 5:13).

Show him the importance of godly friendships and help me encourage him to sustain them.

I pray for strong, peaceful relationships with each of his family members, neighbors, acquaintances, and coworkers. Today I specifically pray for his relationship with (name of person).

Let there be reconciliation and peace where there has been estrangement.

In Jesus' name I pray.

Does your husband have close, mature, believing male friends or mentors who counsel him and encourage his spiritual growth? Does he want men like that in his life? Write out your answers in a prayer asking God for that to become a reality in his life.

MON

SAT

TUES

WED

SUN

THUR

FRI

Pray for your husband to
have godly male friends.
And when he finds them,
give him time to be with them
without criticism. Pray that
those friends will refine him.

Week 30

His Relationships

If you bring your gift to the altar,
and there remember that your brother has something against you,
leave your gift there before the altar, and go your way.
First be reconciled to your brother, and then come and offer your gift.

MATTHEW 5:23-24

Lord, I pray that You would enable my husband to be a forgiving person and not carry grudges or hold things in his heart against others. You've said in Your Word that "he who hates his brother is in darkness and walks in darkness, and does not know where he is going, because the darkness has blinded his eyes" (1 John 2:11).

I pray that my husband would never be blinded by the darkness of unforgiveness, but continually walk in the light of forgiveness. Enable him to love his enemies, bless those who curse him, do good to those who hate him, and pray for those who spitefully use him and persecute him (Matthew 5:44).

I pray that I will be counted as his best friend and the friendship aspect will continue to grow.

In Jesus' name I pray.

Is there any relationship in your husband's life that is strained or broken because of his unforgiveness? Write out a prayer asking God to convict your husband's heart about any need to forgive. Ask God for the same thing concerning you.

MONTH: DATE:

MON

SAT

TUES

WED

SUN

THUR

FRI

Forgiveness is the best
thing for a marriage.
So is having the positive
qualities of other
people rub off on us.

Week 31

His Fatherhood

Whom the LORD loves He corrects,
just as a father the son in whom he delights.

PROVERBS 3:12

Lord, teach (husband's name) to be a good father. Where it was not modeled to him according to Your ways, heal those areas and help him to forgive his dad.

Give him revelation of You and a hunger in his heart to really know You as his heavenly Father. Draw him close to spend time in Your presence so he can become more like You and fully understand Your Father's heart of compassion and love toward him.

Grow that same heart in him for his children, no matter how old he or they are. Help him to balance mercy, judgment, and instruction the way You do. Though You require obedience, You are quick to acknowledge a repentant heart. Make him that way too.

In Jesus' name I pray.

Did your husband have a good father? What does he say his relationship with his father was like? If his father is not around, for whatever reason, what is your husband's attitude toward the father he had? Write out your answers to these questions as a prayer. (For example, "Lord, help my husband to have a good relationship with his father…" Or, "Lord, help my husband to forgive the failures of his father…")

MON

SAT

TUES

WED

SUN

THUR

FRI

Pray that your husband
will gain a right attitude
toward his earthly father
so nothing will stand in
the way of his relationship
with his heavenly Father.

Week 32

His Fatherhood

Children's children are the crown of old men,
and the glory of children is their father.

PROVERBS 17:6

Lord, I pray that my husband will understand how to discipline our children properly. May he never provoke his "children to wrath, but bring them up in the training and admonition of the Lord" (Ephesians 6:4).

I pray we will be united in the rules we set for our children and be in full agreement as to how they are raised.

I pray that there will be no strife or argument over how to handle them and the issues that surround their lives. Give him skills of communication with his children.

I pray he will not be thought of by them as stern, hard, cruel, cold, or abusive, but rather may they see him as kind, softhearted, loving, warm, and affirming.

In Jesus' name I pray.

Does your husband ever feel guilty or as if he has failed as a parent when he sees something wrong with his children? If he does not have children, does he feel a lack because of it? Write out your answers in a prayer about that.

MON

SAT

TUES

WED

SUN

THUR

FRI

The best way for a man
to be a good father
is to get to know his
heavenly Father and
learn to imitate Him.

Prayers for My Husband

Answers to My Prayers

When a man marries, he leaves his father and mother and becomes one with his wife (Matthew 19:5). They are a team, one unit, unified in spirit.

Week 33

His Past

If anyone is in Christ, he is a new creation;
old things have passed away; behold,
all things have become new.

2 Corinthians 5:17

Lord, I pray that You would enable (husband's name) to let go of his past completely. Deliver him from any hold it has on him. Help him to put off his former conduct and habitual ways of thinking about it and be renewed in his mind (Ephesians 4:22-23).

Enlarge his understanding to know that You make all things new (Revelation 21:5).

Show him a fresh, Holy Spirit–inspired way of relating to negative things that have happened. Give him the mind of Christ so that he can clearly discern Your voice from the voices of the past.

When he hears those old voices, enable him to rise up and shut them down with the truth of Your Word.

In Jesus' name I pray.

Is there anything from your husband's past that repeatedly torments him? Is your husband's past a part of his life that he tries to ignore, something from which he learns, or a place where he lives? Write out your answers as a prayer telling God what you want to see Him do in your husband.

MONTH:　　　　　　　　**DATE:**

MON

TUES

WED

THUR

FRI

SAT

SUN

We are to forget "those things which are behind" and reach "forward to those things which are ahead," and we're to "press toward the goal for the prize of the upward call of God in Christ Jesus" (Philippians 3:13-14).

Week 34

His Past

Do not remember the former things, nor consider the things of old.
Behold, I will do a new thing, now it shall spring forth; shall you not know it?
I will even make a road in the wilderness and rivers in the desert.

ISAIAH 43:18-19

Lord, I pray that wherever my husband has experienced rejection in his past, he would not allow that to color what he sees and hears now. Pour forgiveness into his heart so that bitterness, resentment, revenge, and unforgiveness will have no place there. May he regard the past as only a history lesson and not a guide for his daily life.

Wherever his past has become an unpleasant memory, I pray You would redeem it and bring life out of it. Bind up his wounds (Psalm 147:3). Restore his soul (Psalm 23:3).

Help him to release the past so that he will not live in it, but learn from it, break out of it, and move into the future You have for him.

In Jesus' name I pray.

Read Ephesians 4:22-24. Write out these verses as a prayer, inserting your husband's name. Then do the same thing putting in your name.

MONTH: DATE:

MON

TUES

WED

THUR

FRI

SAT

SUN

God can redeem the past
and restore what was
lost. He can make up for
the bad things that have
happened (Psalm 90:15).

Week 35

His Attitude

Be anxious for nothing, but in everything by prayer and supplication,
with thanksgiving, let your requests be made known to God;
and the peace of God, which surpasses all understanding,
will guard your hearts and minds through Christ Jesus.

PHILIPPIANS 4:6-7

Lord, please fill (husband's name) with Your love and peace today. May there be a calmness, serenity, and sense of well-being established in him because his life is God-controlled rather than flesh-controlled. Enable him to walk in his house with a clean and perfect heart before You (Psalm 101:2).

Shine the light of Your Spirit upon him and fill him with Your love. I pray that he will be kind and patient, not selfish or easily provoked.

Release him from anger, unrest, anxiety, concerns, inner turmoil, strife, and pressure.

Enable him to bear all things, believe all things, hope all things, and endure all things (1 Corinthians 13:7).

In Jesus' name I pray.

Does your husband frequently have a bad attitude, or is he usually even-tempered and cheerful? Do events of the day affect your husband's attitude, or is he able to rise above them and cast his cares on the Lord with ease? Write out your answers as a prayer asking God for what you would like to see happen regarding your husband's attitude.

MON

SAT

TUES

WED

SUN

THUR

FRI

We choose our attitude,
just like we choose
to receive the love of
God. We can invite—
or permit—an attitude of
thankfulness to rise in us.

Week 36

His Attitude

Enter into His gates with thanksgiving,
and into His courts with praise.
Be thankful to Him, and bless His name.

PSALM 100:4

Lord, I pray that my husband will have a heart of thanksgiving. May he not be broken in spirit because of sorrow (Proverbs 15:13) but enjoy the continual feast of a merry heart (Proverbs 15:15). Give him a spirit of joy and keep him from growing into a grumpy old man.

Help him to be anxious for nothing, but give thanks in all things so he can know the peace that passes all understanding. May he come to the point of saying, "I have learned in whatever state I am, to be content" (Philippians 4:11).

I say to (husband's name) this day, "The LORD bless you and keep you; the LORD make His face shine upon you, and be gracious to you; the LORD lift up His countenance upon you, and give you peace" (Numbers 6:24-26).

In Jesus' name I pray.

Read Psalm 100:4-5. Does your husband know how to do what is described here? Write out these verses as a prayer for your husband. (For example, "Lord, I pray that my husband will often come to You with an attitude of…")

MONTH: _____   DATE: _____

MON

TUES

WED

THUR

FRI

SAT

SUN

Pray for your husband's
heart to be filled with praise,
thanksgiving, love, and
joy because "a good man
out of the good treasure of
his heart brings forth good
things" (Matthew 12:35).

Prayers for My Husband

Answers to My Prayers

_____
_____
_____
_____
_____
_____
_____
_____
_____
_____
_____
_____
_____
_____
_____
_____
_____
_____
_____

Marriage can be great when two people enter into it with a mutual commitment to keep it strong no matter what.

Week 37

His Marriage

Two are better than one, because they have a good reward for their labor.
For if they fall, one will lift up his companion.
But woe to him who is alone when he falls,
for he has no one to help him up.

ECCLESIASTES 4:9-10

Lord, I pray You would protect our marriage from anything that would harm or destroy it. Shield it from our own selfishness and neglect, from the evil plans and desires of others, and from unhealthy or dangerous situations.

May there be no thoughts of divorce or infidelity in our hearts, and none in our future. Set us free from past hurts and memories, ties from previous relationships, and unrealistic expectations of each other.

I pray that there would be no jealousy in either of us or the low self-esteem that precedes that. Protect us from influences such as alcohol, drugs, gambling, pornography, lust, or obsessions. Let nothing come into our hearts and habits that would threaten our marriage in any way.

In Jesus' name I pray.

Write a statement declaring that you refuse to allow anything to come in and destroy your marriage. Declare to God that you will partner with Him and do whatever it takes as far as you are concerned to see that your marriage becomes all it is supposed to be.

MON

SAT

TUES

WED

SUN

THUR

FRI

We can take a stand against any negative influences in our marriage relationship and know that God has given us authority in His name to back it up.

Week 38

His Marriage

To the married I command, yet not I but the Lord:
A wife is not to depart from her husband.
But even if she does depart, let her remain
unmarried or be reconciled to her husband.
And a husband is not to divorce his wife.

1 Corinthians 7:10-11

Lord, I pray that You would unite my husband and me in a bond of friendship, commitment, generosity, and understanding. Eliminate our immaturity, hostility, or feelings of inadequacy.

Help us to make time for each other alone, to nurture and renew our marriage and remind ourselves of the reasons we were married in the first place.

I pray that (husband's name) will be so committed to You, Lord, that his commitment to me will not waver, no matter what storms come.

I pray that our love for each other will grow stronger every day, so that we will never leave a legacy of divorce to our children.

In Jesus' name I pray.

Read 1 Corinthians 10:12. In light of this Scripture, what should you never assume? How does this Scripture inspire you to keep praying for the strength of your marriage?

MON

TUES

WED

THUR

FRI

SAT

SUN

Don't take your marriage for granted, no matter how great it is. Keep praying for your husband and your marriage so it will never be stolen from you.

Week 39

His Emotions

I waited patiently for the LORD; and He inclined to me, and heard my cry.
He also brought me up out of a horrible pit, out of the miry clay,
and set my feet upon a rock, and established my steps.
He has put a new song in my mouth—praise to our God;
many will see it and fear, and will trust in the LORD.

PSALM 40:1-3

Lord, You have said in Your Word that You redeem our souls when we put our trust in You (Psalm 34:22). I pray that (husband's name) would have faith in You to redeem his soul from negative emotions. May he never be controlled by depression, anger, anxiety, jealousy, hopelessness, fear, or suicidal thoughts.

Specifically, I pray about (area of concern). Deliver him from this and all other controlling emotions (Psalm 40:17).

I know that only You can deliver and heal, but use me as Your instrument of restoration. Help me to not be pulled down with him when he struggles. Enable me instead to rise with understanding and have words to say that will bring life.

In Jesus' name I pray.

Read Proverbs 22:24-25. What can happen when we are frequently around someone with constant negative emotions? (In this example, it's anger.) Do you see from these verses how important it is for your own well-being, as well as your husband's, to pray for his emotions? Write out a prayer asking God to set your husband free from any negative emotions. Describe how his emotions affect yours.

MON

TUES

WED

THUR

FRI

SAT

SUN

The best gift a wife can give in secret to calm her husband's negative emotions is to pray for him.

Week 40

His Emotions

He who trusts in his own heart is a fool,
but whoever walks wisely will be delivered.

PROVERBS 28:26

Lord, I pray that You would give my husband freedom from negative emotions. Release him to share his deepest feelings with me and others who can help.

Liberate him to cry when he needs to and not bottle his emotions inside. At the same time, give him the gift of laughter and ability to find humor in even serious situations.

Teach him to take his eyes off his circumstances and trust in You, regardless of how he is feeling. Give him patience to possess his soul and the ability to take charge of it (Luke 21:19).

Anoint him with "the oil of joy" (Isaiah 61:3), refresh him with Your Spirit, and set him free from any destructive emotions this day.

In Jesus' name I pray.

Read Psalm 34:1-4. From these verses, what is it we should be doing to combat anger, depression, and fear? How often are we to praise Him? Write out your answers as a prayer. (For example, "Lord, I pray that my husband will have a desire to praise You at all times and…")

MONTH: DATE:

MON

SAT

TUES

WED

SUN

THUR

FRI

Don't stand by and
watch your husband
be manipulated by his
emotions. Freedom may
be just a prayer away.

Prayers for My Husband

Answers to My Prayers

Pray that your husband will stop being controlled by his emotions and instead be controlled by the Holy Spirit.

Week 41

His Walk

LORD, who may abide in Your tabernacle?
Who may dwell in Your holy hill?
He who walks uprightly, and works righteousness,
and speaks the truth in his heart.

PSALM 15:1-2

O Lord, I know the way of man is not in himself; it is not in man who walks to direct his own steps" (Jeremiah 10:23). Therefore, Lord, I pray that You would direct my husband's steps. Lead him in Your light and teach him Your way so that he will walk in Your truth.

I pray he would have a deeper walk with You and an ever-progressing hunger for Your Word. May Your presence be like a delicacy he never ceases to crave.

Lead him on Your path and make him quick to confess when he strays from it. Reveal to him any hidden sin that would hinder him from walking rightly before You. May he experience deep repentance when he doesn't live in obedience to Your laws.

In Jesus' name I pray.

Read Psalm 84:11. What are the rewards for those who live God's way? Write out your answer as a prayer for your husband. (For example, "Lord, I pray You would help my husband to always _____ because You have promised to…")

MONTH:

DATE:

MON

TUES

WED

THUR

FRI

SAT

SUN

Pray that your husband is guided
by God's Holy Spirit. Pray that
he stays on the path by having
faith in God's Word, a heart for
obedience, and deep repentance
for any actions he takes that
are not God's will for his life.

Week 42

His Walk

He who walks righteously and speaks uprightly,
he who despises the gain of oppressions,
who gestures with his hands, refusing bribes,
who stops his ears from hearing of bloodshed,
and shuts his eyes from seeing evil: he will dwell on high;
his place of defense will be the fortress of rocks;
bread will be given him, his water will be sure.

Isaiah 33:15-16

Lord, I pray that You would create a clean heart in my husband and renew a steadfast spirit within him. Don't cast him away from Your presence, and do not take Your Holy Spirit from him (Psalm 51:10-11).

Your Word says that those who are in the flesh cannot please You (Romans 8:8). I pray that You will enable (husband's name) to walk in the Spirit and not in the flesh and thereby keep himself "from the paths of the destroyer" (Psalm 17:4).

As he walks in the Spirit, may he bear the fruit of the Spirit, which is love, joy, peace, patience, kindness, goodness, faithfulness, gentleness, and self-control (Galatians 5:22-23 NASB).

In Jesus' name I pray.

Do you trust your husband to walk righteously, or do you fear he can be easily led off the right path? Write out your answer as a prayer telling God how you feel about this and why. Then pray for your husband accordingly.

MONTH:

DATE:

MON

TUES

WED

THUR

FRI

SAT

SUN

God desires that your husband's
every step be led by Him
(Galatians 5:25) so He can
walk with him daily and grow
your husband into His image.
A husband who walks with
God is desirable in every way.

Week 43

His Talk

Let no corrupt word proceed out of your mouth,
but what is good for necessary edification,
that it may impart grace to the hearers.

EPHESIANS 4:29

Lord, I pray Your Holy Spirit would guard my husband's mouth so that he will speak only words that edify and bring life. Help him to not be a grumbler, complainer, a user of foul language, or one who destroys with his words, but be disciplined enough to keep his conversation godly.

Your Word says a man who desires a long life must keep his tongue from evil and his lips from speaking deceit (Psalm 34:12-13).

Show him how to do that. Fill him with Your love so that out of the overflow of his heart will come words that build up and not tear down. Work that in my heart as well.

In Jesus' name I pray.

Read Ephesians 4:29-31. Write out these verses as a prayer over your husband.

MONTH: _____   DATE: _____

MON

TUES

WED

THUR

FRI

SAT

SUN

"Whoever guards his mouth and tongue keeps his soul from troubles" (Proverbs 21:23). Ask God to help you and your husband to be careful about the words you both speak.

Week 44

His Talk

The words of a wise man's mouth are gracious,
but the lips of a fool shall swallow him up.

Ecclesiastes 10:12

Lord, may Your Spirit of love reign in the words my husband and I speak to each other so that we don't miscommunicate or wound one another. Help us to show each other respect, speak words that encourage, share our feelings openly, and come to mutual agreements without strife.

Lord, You've said in Your Word that when two agree, You are in their midst (Matthew 18:20). I pray that the reverse be true as well—that You will be in our midst so that we two can agree.

Let the words of our mouths and the meditations of our hearts be acceptable in Your sight, O Lord, our strength and our Redeemer (Psalm 19:14).

In Jesus' name I pray.

Read Proverbs 15:23. What can we derive from the words we speak? Does your husband need more of that in his life? Do you? Write out your answers in a prayer. (For example, "Lord, Your Word says that by the words we speak we can receive…")

MONTH: DATE:

MON

TUES

WED

THUR

FRI

SAT

SUN

Pray for the Holy Spirit
to fill your husband's
heart with love, peace,
and joy; and teach him
new ways to talk that
always glorify the Lord.

Week 45

His Repentance

Search me, O God, and know my heart;
try me, and know my anxieties;
and see if there is any wicked way in me,
and lead me in the way everlasting.

PSALM 139:23-24

Lord, I pray that You would convict my husband of any error in his life. Let there be "nothing covered that will not be revealed, and hidden that will not be known" (Matthew 10:26).

Cleanse him from any secret sins and teach him to be a person who is quick to confess when he is wrong (Psalm 19:12).

Help him to recognize his mistakes. Bring him to full repentance before You. Let his suffering come from a remorseful heart and not because the crushing hand of the enemy has found an opening into his life through unconfessed sin. Lord, I know that humility must come before honor (Proverbs 15:33). Take away all pride and work into his soul a humility of heart so that he will receive the honor You have for him.

In Jesus' name I pray.

Do you feel your husband moves fully in the steps of confession, repentance, and asking forgiveness? With which step does he have the most difficulty? The least difficulty? Write out your answers in a prayer about this.

MON

TUES

WED

THUR

FRI

SAT

SUN

Pray for your husband to be convicted of his sin, to humbly confess it before God, and then turn from his error and cease to do it.

Prayers for My Husband

Answers to My Prayers

Repentance is a working of
God's grace, and you can
pray for it to be worked
in your husband's heart.

Week 46

His Deliverance

The LORD is my rock and my fortress and my deliverer;
my God, my strength, in whom I will trust;
my shield and the horn of my salvation, my stronghold.
I will call upon the LORD, who is worthy to be praised;
so shall I be saved from my enemies.

PSALM 18:2-3

Lord, You have said to call upon You in the day of trouble and You will deliver us (Psalm 50:15). I call upon You now and ask that You would work deliverance in my husband's life. Deliver him from anything that binds him. Set him free from (name a specific thing). Lift him away from the hands of the enemy (Psalm 31:15).

Bring him to a place of understanding where he can recognize the work of evil and cry out to You for help. If the deliverance he prays for isn't immediate, keep him from discouragement and help him to be confident that You have begun a good work in him and will complete it (Philippians 1:6).

Give him the certainty that even in his most hopeless state, when he finds it impossible to change anything, You, Lord, can change everything.

In Jesus' name I pray.

Read Psalm 91:14-15. Often, if we simply set our sights on the Lord, have a heart for Him, and live His way, we will see deliverance happen. How could you pray these verses over your husband, trusting that deliverance will happen for him? Write out your answers as a prayer for your husband. (For example, "Lord, I pray that my husband will know You and love You in a deep way and learn to…")

MONTH: DATE:

MON

SAT

TUES

WED

SUN

THUR

FRI

How glorious to embrace
the certainty that when
there seems to be no way
out, God can miraculously
lift us up and away from
whatever is seeking to
entrap us (Psalm 25:15).

Week 47

His Obedience

My son, do not forget my law, but let your heart keep my commands;
for length of days and long life and peace they will add to you.
Let not mercy and truth forsake you; bind them around your neck,
write them on the tablet of your heart.

PROVERBS 3:1-3

Lord, You have said in Your Word that if we regard iniquity in our hearts, You will not hear (Psalm 66:18). I want You to hear my prayers, so I ask You to reveal where there is any disobedience in my life, especially with regard to my husband.

Show me if I'm selfish, unloving, critical, angry, resentful, unforgiving, or bitter toward him. If so, I confess it as sin and ask for Your forgiveness.

I pray that You would also give (husband's name) a desire to live in obedience to Your laws and Your ways. Reveal and uproot anything he willingly gives place to that is not of You. Help him to bring every thought and action under Your control.

Remind him to do good; speak evil of no one; and be peaceable, gentle, and humble (Titus 3:1-2).

In Jesus' name I pray.

One of the best ways to learn how God wants us to live is to read His Word. Does your husband read the Bible regularly? Does he get good Bible teaching? Write out a prayer below asking God to open your husband's heart to an ever-increasing knowledge of the truth of His Word.

126

MON

TUES

WED

THUR

FRI

SAT

SUN

Keep praying that your husband will hear the voice of God speaking to his heart, and that he has the strength, courage, and motivation to act on what he hears.

Week 48

His Self-Image

We all, with unveiled face,
beholding as in a mirror the glory of the Lord,
are being transformed into the same image from glory to glory,
just as by the Spirit of the Lord.

2 CORINTHIANS 3:18

Lord, I pray that (husband's name) will find his identity in You. Help him to understand his worth through Your eyes and by Your standards. May he recognize the unique qualities You've placed in him and be able to appreciate them.

Enable him to see himself the way You see him, understanding that "You have made him a little lower than the angels, and You have crowned him with glory and honor. You have made him to have dominion over the works of Your hands; You have put all things under his feet" (Psalm 8:5-6).

Quiet the voices that tell him otherwise and give him ears to hear Your voice telling him that it will not be his perfection that gets him through life successfully—it will be Yours.

In Jesus' name I pray.

Part of being accepted by other people has to do with accepting who we are in the Lord first. Do you feel your husband accepts himself or is he hard on himself? Write out your answer to that question as a prayer asking God to help your husband receive love and acceptance from the Lord and find his identity in Him.

MON

TUES

WED

THUR

FRI

SAT

SUN

Your husband will never see who he really is until he sees who God really is. Pray that he finds his true identity.

Week 49

His Faith

Let him ask in faith, with no doubting,
for he who doubts is like a wave of the sea driven and tossed by the wind.
For let not that man suppose that he will receive anything from the Lord;
he is a double-minded man, unstable in all his ways.

JAMES 1:6-8

Lord, I pray that You will give (husband's name) an added measure of faith today. Enlarge his ability to believe in You, Your Word, Your promises, Your ways, and Your power. Put a longing in his heart to talk with You and hear Your voice.

Give him an understanding of what it means to bask in Your presence and not just ask for things. May he seek You, rely totally upon You, be led by You, put You first, and acknowledge You in everything he does. Lord, You have said in Your Word that "whatever is not from faith is sin" (Romans 14:23).

May my husband be free from the sin of doubt in his life.

In Jesus' name I pray.

Read Matthew 17:19-20. Write out a prayer asking God to help your husband develop the kind of faith that moves mountains so that what Jesus describes will happen to him.

MONTH:　　　　　　　　　　　　　**DATE:**

MON

TUES

WED

THUR

FRI

SAT

SUN

There is nothing in your husband's life that can't be conquered or positively affected with an added measure of faith in God.

Prayers for My Husband

Answers to My Prayers

Every day is a walk of faith. Jesus said, "According to your faith let it be done to you" (Matthew 9:29). Our faith will determine our outcome.

Week 50

His Hearing

Whoever listens to me will dwell safely,
and will be secure, without fear of evil.

PROVERBS 1:33

Lord, Your Word says that "he who has ears to hear, let him hear!" (Matthew 11:15). I pray You would give my husband ears to hear You speaking to his heart. Help him to "incline" his ears toward You at all times (Proverbs 22:17). Enable him to listen as You speak to him through Your Word and through Your Holy Spirit impressing his heart and mind. Open his ears to not only hear You but to hear me as well. Enable me to hear from You at all times and to continually grow in wisdom and discernment. When I need to say something important to him, prepare his heart to receive it without pride, rejection, or disregard for the fact that You have made us to be one.

In Jesus' name I pray.

Read John 8:43. Why didn't the people understand Jesus? In light of this Scripture, write out a prayer for both you and your husband to be able to hear God speaking to you from His Word.

MON

SAT

TUES

WED

SUN

THUR

FRI

Pray for your husband to hear God's voice to his soul, and to hear from his soul mate—the person with whom he has become one— the person who may also go over the cliff with him. You!

Week 51

His Future

I know the thoughts that I think toward you,
says the LORD, thoughts of peace and not of evil,
to give you a future and a hope.

JEREMIAH 29:11

Lord, I pray that You would give (husband's name) a vision for his future. Help him to understand that Your plans for him are good and not evil—to give him a future and a hope (Jeremiah 29:11).

Fill him with the knowledge of Your will in all wisdom and spiritual understanding that he may have a walk worthy of You, fully pleasing You, being fruitful in every good work and increasing in the knowledge of You (Colossians 1:9-10).

May he live by the leading of the Holy Spirit and not walk in doubt and fear of what may happen. Help him to mature and grow in You daily, submitting to You all his dreams and desires, knowing that "the things which are impossible with men are possible with God" (Luke 18:27).

In Jesus' name I pray.

Does your husband have a vision for the future? Even though he may not know specifics about his future, does he have a sense of the direction he's going in and feel good about it? Write out your answers in a prayer asking God to give him that vision.

MONTH:　　　　　　　　　　　**DATE:**

MON

TUES

WED

THUR

FRI

SAT

SUN

The Lord is the giver of vision; pray that your husband looks to Him for it. With God, his future is secure.

Week 52

His Future

One thing I have desired of the Lord, that will I seek:
that I may dwell in the house of the Lord all the days of my life,
to behold the beauty of the Lord, and to inquire in His temple.

Psalm 27:4

Lord, I pray that (husband's name) will always conduct himself in a way that invests in his future. Keep him from losing his sense of purpose and fill him with hope for his future as an "anchor of the soul, both sure and steadfast" (Hebrews 6:19).

Give him "his heart's desire" (Psalm 21:2) and keep him fresh and flourishing and bearing fruit into old age (Psalm 92:13-14).

And when it comes time for him to leave this earth and go to be with You, may he have such a strong vision for his eternal future that it makes his transition smooth, painless, and accompanied by peace and joy. Until that day, I pray he will find the vision for his future in You.

In Jesus' name I pray.

What do you think concerns your husband most about his future? Now ask him. Write out a prayer regarding everything your husband mentioned being concerned about for his future. Tell him you are going to be praying for each one of those concerns.

MON

SAT

TUES

WED

SUN

THUR

FRI

God can restore vision where it has been lost. He can give hope to dream again. He can bring His truth to bear upon the lies of discouragement. He can give assurance of a promising future. Prayer is the avenue through which He can accomplish it.

Prayers for My Husband